# LOWE'S
# MOTOR SPEEDWAY
## a Weekend at the Track

By *KATHY PERSINGER*

SPORTS
PUBLISHING
L.L.C.

# LOWE'S
## MOTOR SPEEDWAY
### a Weekend at the Track

Coordinating Editor:
**Lynnette A. Bogard**

Interior Design, Project Manager, Photo Imaging & Dust Jacket Design:
**Kerri Baker**

Publisher:
**Peter Bannon**

Senior Managing Editors:
**Joseph J. Bannon, Jr. and Susan Moyer**

Art Director:
**K. Jeffery Higgerson**

Dust Jacket and Photo Imaging Assistance:
**Christine Mohrbacher**

Copy Editor:
**Cynthia L. McNew**

All Photos:
**Harold Hinson**

ISBN 1-58261-662-0

**Sports Publishing L.L.C.**
*www.sportspublishingllc.com*

FOREWORD

## By H. A. "Humpy" Wheeler

Upon its opening in 1960, this massive structure became the center point of the development of what is now the billion-dollar stock car racing industry in the Charlotte area.

Along with Atlanta, Darlington and Daytona, it ushered in the superspeedway era of NASCAR.

The great success of this speedway was the result of inspiration, creativity, dedication and just plain ol' elbow grease of many, many people. Bruton Smith and I have gotten entirely too much credit for this success. But it was the previous managers, the architects, the engineers, the publicists, the ticket sellers, the media, the police, the fire and rescue workers, and last but not least the plumbers, the electricians and the skilled tradesmen who together enable massive crowds to see one of racing's great spectacles.

But the fans don't come to see us. They come to see the world's best stock car drivers challenge this mile-and-a-half quad-oval.

Every time the green flag drops, I remember the great ones who performed here ... guys like Fireball Roberts, Curtis Turner, A. J. Foyt, Richard Petty, Joe Lee Johnson, Fearless Freddie Lorenzen, David Pearson, Darrell Waltrip, Cale Yarborough, Lee Roy Yarbrough, Buddy and Buck Baker, Harry Gant and the other great drivers who have since hung up their helmets.

And we can't forget the ladies who made history here, especially Janet Guthrie, Lilian Vandiver Hooper, and Patti Moise.

They furnished the excitement, the drama and the great racing that made this place.

All we did was furnish the stage and throw a little color on it.

# TABLE OF CONTENTS

# ACKNOWLEDGMENTS

In October 2002, I took my three children to the Grand National race at Lowe's Motor Speedway, a family day out together.

The staff at the track, from the woman at the ticket window, to the ushers, to the people who sold the soft drinks and lemonade all greeted us with a smile, a pleasant voice and a general sense that they truly enjoyed their jobs.

We had good seats in a friendly crowd, and though our car didn't win, everyone left satisfied.

Such is the kind of production the LMS staff tries to attain, so when the people at Sports Publishing asked about a book on the track, it was a welcome request.

I'd like to thank track president and general manager H. A. "Humpy" Wheeler for his time, his humor, and his stories about being a part of one of the most popular NASCAR tracks in the country. He is a gift to the world of stock car racing.

Thanks to Jerry Gappens, the vice president of public relations and promotions at the track, who seems to know everything that's going on, even before it happens. His insight and his knowledge of the speedway are priceless.

No race at Lowe's would be complete without input from Jay Howard, owner of JHE Production Group in Concord, North Carolina, which partners with Wheeler to put on the entertaining prerace shows for which the course is famous. Howard's wit and imagination are an integral part of making LMS tick.

Thanks to Lynnette Bogard of Sports Publishing for her guidance and encouragement.

And, finally, to my children—Christopher, Sarah and Tyler—for their support and their love.

*—Kathy Persinger*

I't's hot. It doesn't matter if it's May or October; the impression is that it will be hot, but you bring a jacket anyway.

And you prepare, because fans know traffic takes forever along I-85, along N.C. 29 and N.C. 49, along the side streets that aren't really shortcuts after all, and the motorcade inching toward the race track is moving at a collective speed of five mph.

On race days at Lowe's Motor Speedway, just north of Charlotte, North Carolina, the people who are magnetically drawn to the track, like a mandatory summons, and the people who work there for a few days to hawk allegiance-specific stuff for a quick buck turn tiny Concord, the place's real hometown, into the state's fourth largest city.

It smells of greasy outdoor grills, of exhaust and smoke, and of sweat and yesterday's drained beverages. And it dances in synchronized camaraderie to the tune of country music CDs and Motor Racing Network radio shows and some guy in a tent who thought, well, yeah, bringing his guitar along would be a good idea.

Leading up to the big moment, the fans, some of whom have been there for days, find ways to deal with anticipation—a preschooler in an oversized bike helmet zips around a tent camp across the street on a four-wheeler, at a speed of not too much, pretending he's Jeff Gordon in the final lap. A man old enough to have accepted fate by now covers himself with Dale Earnhardt clothes and flies a "3" banner from his temporary home, as he sips from a "3" mug and waves a tiny "3" flag.

The impromptu culture is divided by whose name is on your T-shirt and, in the infield, by what section—tent, camper (turns one and two), or motor home (turns three and four)—you choose for your weekend ZIP code.

But when the cars roar, when it's finally time, the people are one. The toddler, the blue-collar worker, the banker's child—they are drawn together by the bumper-stickered rainbow swirling around them, challenging a 1.5-mile quad-oval of concrete, a 40-foot-wide path that will lead some to celebrate, some to stomp away in frustration.

This book tells a little about Lowe's Motor Speedway, which hosts two races each year on the NASCAR Winston Cup tour. It talks about the people who run the track, some of the crazy stories they have to tell, and about what it's like to be the first facility in this Sunday sport to be named for a sponsor, not its location.

And we go inside a race day—the preparations, the technical details, the whole cornucopia of presenting a NASCAR stock car race to the world.

Welcome to Lowe's Motor Speedway, Concord, N.C., 28027. We hope you enjoy the ride.

*—Kathy Persinger*

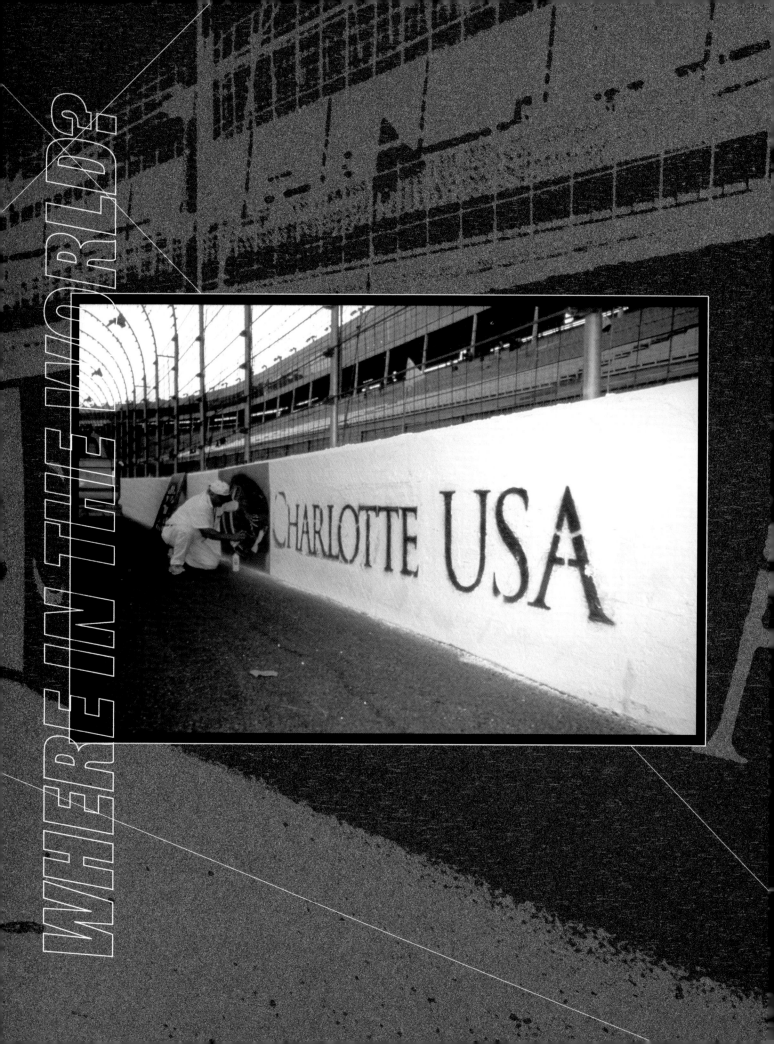

# Where in the World?

The stock car race tracks of Charlotte, North Carolina are not, never were, never have been, within the city limits of Charlotte.

In the beginning, drivers navigated a 1.25-mile wooden oval in the Charlotte suburb of Pineville, population back then, in 1924, only a few hundred (a 1900 census claims 585 residents). The track wasn't much more than a slow circle of boards, with 40-degree banked turns, plopped down on rich dirt flavored with Confederate clay. Bordered by dark wooden fence rails and wobbly bleachers, it was a place for wives and youngsters and extra kin to gather on Saturday nights in Southern summers.

The track was built by a guy named Jack Prince, at a cost of $38,000. At that time, in 1924, the racers who came before the National Association for Stock Car Auto Racing were riding the circuit powered by jazzed-up sedans and showroom family automobiles, done proud in back-yard garages late at night, after

11

the men, the drivers, crew and hangers-on—had finished work at the cotton gin, or Highland Mill, on what later would be North Davidson Street in downtown Charlotte.

Come Saturday, they'd tow their cars out to the wooden oval and let 'em roll. A man named Earl Cooper was announced as the first winner there, when the first flag fell on October 24, 1924, but someone didn't like that much, and the tapes were reviewed and the winner changed to Tommy Milton.

That same day, tragedy struck when driver Earl Antersberg was killed. By and by, the wood track gave way to Southern sun and nature, and by 1927 the surface had deteriorated so much that the owners decided not to fix it. The track closed on September 19, 1927.

Today, Pineville, a small suburb southeast of Charlotte that keeps an old-fashioned charm, is up to 3,500 residents in a land area of 7.2 square kilometers.

On June 19, 1960, a new track, this one named Charlotte Motor Speedway, held its first race—in Concord, outside the Charlotte and Mecklenburg County limits, next door in Cabarrus County. Joe Lee Johnson was the winner.

In 1999, the track became the first in the country to be named for a corporate sponsor—Lowe's—and took on the name of the home improvement warehouse giant becoming Lowe's Motor Speedway. It is now the flagship track of Speedway Motorsports, Inc., the first publicly traded motorsports company on the New York Stock Exchange,

and hosts more major events than any motorsports facility in the world.

Naming the speedway for a sponsor had its benefits, but it also tugged at the emotions of some employees who had long identified the track with its location.

"What happened was, we're a part of Speedway Motorsports, and there's obviously pressure to do well," says Jerry Gappens, the track's vice president of public relations and promotions. "So we have to have a good return for stockholders and investors. Football and basketball came up with this, to attach naming rights to a facility."

The tracks in Atlanta, Las Vegas, Texas and Sears Point, California (named in 2002 for Infineon Technologies, a semicon-

ductor manufacturing company) were other candidates for corporate sponsorship. Texas Motor Speedway was a frontrunner, with its name not already tied to a city. But Lowe's, which is based in North Carolina, got the deal.

"It was a blockbuster announcement," Gappens says. "They thought it would make more sense to put a name on our facility from a company that's right here in our back yard. We get more than one million visitors a year, and they have a 10-year naming right to the facility. It was big news."

Still, for employees and those who could recall the track's creation more than 40 years before, there was a hollow separation.

"It was kind of a mixed emotion for employees of the speedway. Even though we're in Concord, our identity is that of Charlotte Motor Speedway," Gappens says. "It's like a college—there's a lot of pride associated with your university. But at the same time, it was exciting to know that there were these marketing dollars that would open up some more avenues to expand and grow. Now, that partnership has kind of found its way, and we've been able to do some of the things that we've envisioned."

It's come a long way from a time when the track almost flunked its first test. When chairman Bruton Smith was looking to build Charlotte Motor Speedway back in 1959, he already was thinking ahead in terms of development and poplulation—he wanted a site within 15 miles of the intersection of Trade Street and Tryon Street, commonly called "The Square," in the heart of downtown Charlotte. The speedway, it turns out, is, in a straight line, 12 miles away from the Square.

Partnering wih the late driver Curtis Turner, a Virginia native with money from the lumber business, Smith, of Oakboro, N.C., used his funding from his career as an automobile dealer and short-track promoter to carve the 1.5-mile superspeedway.

"He felt it was important to have that connection with the metropolitan area," Gappens says. "And he had to find property he could afford. This tract of land now has 2,000 acres available to us, 1,100 of which we own." But Smith's dream track proved to be, literally, a rocky road, filled with hard stone and granite. "They had to do a lot of blasting, to get the track laid in there, and that drove up the construction prices out of their budget," Gappens says.

The result was that naughty word in business—Chapter 11 bankruptcy. In 1961, with money tight and ticket sales low, the track filed for reorganization. Smith dove into the Ford Motor Company dealership program and started purchasing stock in CMS. By 1975, he was a majority stockholder and had regained control of the speedway's day-to-day operations.

"One of the first things he did," Gappens says, "was to hire Humpy Wheeler."

H. A. "Humpy" Wheeler became general manager, and the two, through the years, have become both marketing entrepreneurs and with Wheeler's imagination, practical jokers in terms of promotions.

With Wheeler overseeing the progress, grandstands were added, and, in 1988, the Smith Tower opened—a 135,000-square-foot facility with offices, a gift shop and the exclusive Speedway Club dining and entertainment venture.

In 1984, the speedway began offering year-round living quarters when 40 condominiums were built above turn one. Twelve more were added in 1991.

"People laughed," at the condo idea, Gappens said. "Well, they needed to build more grandstands, and the proceeds from the condos would go into the infrastructure. [Talk show host] David Letterman [who has a history of speeding tickets] even called about buying one. He said it would be nice to live in a place without a speed limit out front."

Letterman didn't buy a condo, but the first 32 units sold out at prices ranging from $125,000 to $500,000, Gappens says. Penthouses are up to $1.2 million.

While the condos, which range from 1,200 square feet to 1,700 square feet, don't have any permanent residents, all units are sold and are used by drivers' companies or others who occupy them to entertain clients, or as a home away from home during race weeks. Teresa Earnhardt owns one. So does Bobby Allison.

Another Smith-Wheeler innovation came in 1992, when a $1.7 million, 1,200-fixture permanent lighting system was installed, making the track the first to host NASCAR racing at night. The system, developed by Musco Lighting of Oskaloosa, Iowa, uses panels along the track that reflect light to simulate daylight without glare.

In 1994, the track added a $1 million, 20,000-square-foot garage area.

Also built were a sixth-tenths-mile karting track in the infield and, in 2000, a four-tenths-mile state-of-the-art dirt track for World of Outlaws sprint cars, motorcycles and monster trucks.

The track also hosts the FasTrack Driving School and the Richard Petty Driving Experience.

Movies have been filmed at the track, including the Tom Cruise race flick *Days of Thunder*, as well as country music videos.

In 1995, 10,000 seats and 20 executive suites were added in turn four, and in 1997, the Diamond Tower Terrace grandstand, which seats 26,000, was opened on the backstretch. In May 1998, 11,000 seats were added to the terrace, and 10,860 seats were added to the Ford grandstand on the frontstretch in May 2000, bringing the seating capacity to 167,000.

The facility has become an integral part of life in Concord, N.C.

"We are involved in the community," Gappens says. "We have a presence in this community."

# CHAPTER TWO

# The Ringleaders

## O. BRUTON SMITH

**Lowe's Motor Speedway Founder and Chief Executive Officer**

Olin Bruton Smith, one of NASCAR's most powerful men, grew up on a farm near Oakboro, North Carolina, a small town in Stanly County, northeast of Charlotte. Oakboro, a map dot encircled by the towns of Red Cross, Big Lick and Aquadale, is where Smith founded his automotive empires.

In the 1950s, he became a car dealer and took to promoting various NASCAR events. He was known in the league's infancy as a promoter who paid well and put the fans' needs first at the tracks he leased around North Carolina.

**O. Bruton Smith**

He built his first race track, Charlotte Motor Speedway, in 1959 and hosted its first race in June 1960—a 600-miler. The speedway was a success, and large crowds came, but it eventually fell into Chapter 11 reorganization. It later became the first North Carolina company to recover from that filing.

During those years, Smith took on business interests in Texas and Illinois, all the while purchasing stock in CMS. He started working at car dealerships, became a Ford executive, and by 1975 was the majority stockholder in his speedway. The daily operations were once again his to control.

Smith founded Speedway Motorsports, Inc. in 1974 and in 1975 made it the first motorsports company to trade on the New York Stock Exchange. Today, SMI operates six tracks—Atlanta Motor Speedway, Bristol Motor Speedway, Lowe's, Las Vegas Motor Speedway, Infineon Raceway and Texas Motor Speedway. SMI subsidiary Finish Line Events provides event concessions and souvenir services to tracks.

In 1996, Smith was named to the Forbes 400 list as one of the wealthiest people in the United States. In 1997, he organized his automotive interests as Sonic Automotive, which owns

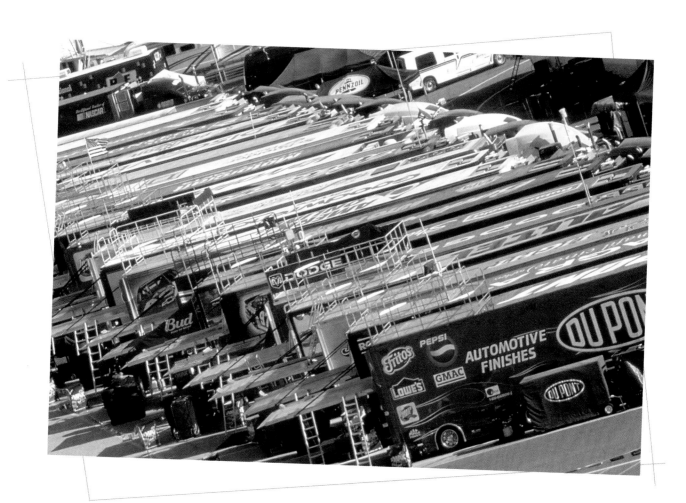

and operates more than 170 car dealerships and 30 collision centers in the nation, and placed it on the New York Stock Exchange.

Smith's other interests have made him majority owner of a Class A minor-league baseball team, the Kannapolis (N.C.) Intimidators, nicknamed for Kannapolis native Dale Earnhardt. He founded Speedway Children's Charities in 1984, a non-profit organization that has raised more than $5 million. In 1997, Smith was honored with the NASCAR Award of Excellence for his work with children's charities.

H.A. "Humpy" Wheeler

# H. A. "HUMPY" WHEELER

**Lowe's President and General Manager**

"Humpy," says Jerry Gappens, LMS vice president of public relations and promotions, "is kind of a combination of Walt Disney, Don King and P. T. Barnum. ... P. T. Barnum with his three-ring circus, Don King with his ability for creating attention, and Walt Disney for his way of looking into the future. And Humpy's got the quality of all three."

H. A. "Humpy" Wheeler has been president and general manager of the speedway since 1975, when he was hired by Bruton Smith. Known for his outlandish promotions and unusual prerace shows, he is a reason LMS is called one of the world's leading sports facilities.

Wheeler was born in tiny Belmont, North Carolina, and went to the University of South Carolina on a football scholarship, graduating in 1961 with a journalism degree. He also boxed in college and as an amateur, going 40-2 in Golden Gloves competitions. He was inducted into the Carolinas Boxing Hall of Fame in 1992.

Wheeler used his degree to find work as a sportswriter and television director and spent time as a real estate manager and dirt track operator. He also was director of racing for the Firestone Tire & Rubber Co.

Now on the board of directors for Speedway Motorsports, Inc., Wheeler is a director of Atlanta Motor Speedway and a vice president and director of Bristol Motor Speedway, Infineon Raceway and Texas Motor Speedway. He also is on the boards of Belmont Abbey College, the National Motorsports Council and the Governor's Sports Commission. He has been active with the Charlotte Convention & Visitors Bureau, Charlotte Catholic Services and the Boy Scouts of America.

His awards include National Auto Racing Promoter of the Year, the Charles J. Parker award for the person contributing the most to tourism in the state of North Carolina, and the Bill France Award for outstanding achievement in auto racing, given by Pocono Raceway.

Wheeler and his wife, Pat, live on Lake Norman in Cornelius, North Carolina.

**Mike Helton**

# CHAPTER THREE

# Busy, Busy, Busy

There is no off season at Lowe's Motor Speedway.

There are off days, generally during the Christmas season, but racing, and racing events, are year-round. And it isn't just cars. Movies have been filmed there (see Tom Cruise's *Days of Thunder*) and commercials, and then there's the Richard Petty Driving Experience, in which people can buy a ride in, or a chance to drive, an actual stock car. In Concord, it's more than the Coca-Cola 600 in May and the UAW-GM 500 in October. It's one thing after another.

"The May race [the Coca-Cola 600], we start to focus on that as soon as the October race is completed," says the track's Jerry Gappens. "And ticket renewals go out in June, and they have until July the previous year [to get tickets]. When we really roll up our sleeves is when we get back in January. It seems like someone turns on the racing switch when Daytona starts up in February. It really intensifies what we're doing, as far as preparing."

Race weeks in May begin with The Winston, the All-Star three-part dash that pits Winston Cup winners against one another under the lights. Prior to that is the Winston Open qualifying race and an ARCA event.

The Winston debuted at what then was Charlotte Motor Speedway in 1985, moved to Atlanta for one year, and returned to Charlotte for good in 1987. After The Winston was again awarded to LMS for 2003, there was talk of moving it to a different venue in coming years. But track president and general manager Humpy Wheeler told an area newspaper, "In the past, Charlotte and the surrounding communities have put their best foot forward in hosting the NCAA Final Four and the NBA All-Star Game. We're looking for that type of effort for The Winston and plan to turn this into the greatest All-Star event in all of major sports."

Pole night is accompanied by a Legends Car event, a Goody's Dash Series race and a Busch Series 300 race. And all the while, as fans accumulate at the track, a street festival is being held in uptown Charlotte, with race vendors, food booths, games for children and, annually, a visit from the Budweiser Clydesdales.

Wheeler estimates that The Winston and race weeks in May bring nearly $100 million into the economy of the Charlotte area. By the time the Coca-Cola 600 rolls out on Sunday night, more than 200,000 fans will have spent time and money in the Charlottte-Concord region.

In October, pole night for the UAW-GM 500 is accompanied by the ARCA/ReMAX Series season finale. Then there's the Busch Series race on Saturday, an event that typically attracts several Winston Cup drivers, and "Happy Hour," the last practice before the big race, which, starting in 2003, is a Saturday night event.

Outside the main course at Lowe's, the four-tenths-mile dirt track hosts the Charlotte Outlaw Championship, in which open-wheeled sprint cars of the World of Outlaws make two stops each season. The 900-horsepower winged racers roll in for one event accompanying the May race and one in October.

"We have approximately 150 full-time employees at the speedway. It's a year-round process," says Gappens.

"On event weekends, it will swell to 5,000 people, with volunteers and event-time help. Of course, pretty much after the first race is complete, we get ready for the next race. We have two auto fairs, one in the spring and one in the fall, so the track is literally being used all the time. We have 10 to 12 major spectator weekends that we're always working on."

Many visiting ticket holders choose to make their stay in the Charlotte area an extended visit. There are dozens of NASCAR teams headquartered near the track and in adjacent Mooresville, where fans can visit the shops, and Lowe's offers speedway tours that let people experience the Winston Cup garages, pit road, Victory Circle and take a ride in a van around the track.

The track's Winston Gift Shop has one of the largest selections of track memorabilia on the East Coast.

# On the road again...

## LOWE'S SUPERSPEEDWAY

May 4 _____

May 16 _____

May 17 _____

October 10 _____

October 11 _____

October 30, 31 _____

November 1, 2 _____

November 28 _____

# A typical year, based on the 2003 schedule, for the tracks of Lowe's Motor Speedway.

_____ *Cinco de Mayo Latino Festival*

_____ *The Winston Pole Night, Hardee's 200 NASCAR Craftsman Truck Series*

_____ *EasyCare Vehicle Service Contracts 100—NASCAR Goody's Dash Series*
*Also: The Winston & The Winston Open*

_____ *Busch Series 300 race*

_____ *UAW-GM Quality 500 NASCAR Winston Cup Series race*

_____ *North American Karting Championship*

_____ *North American Karting Championship*

_____ *Souvenir Blowout*

DIRT TRACK

April 3, 4, 5, 6

August 30, 31

September 11, 12, 13, 14

October 24, 25, 26

CAR SHOWS

## Food Lion Auto Fair

## Southern All-Ford Centennial Celebration

## Food Lion Auto Fair

## GoodGuys Southeastern Nationals

GETTING THERE

GETTING THERE

DRIVING

**Charlotte/ Douglas International Airport**

**5501 Josh Birmingham Parkway**

**Charlotte, N.C. 28208**

**(704) 359-4013 (phone)**

**(704) 359-4910 (fax)**

**Concord Regional Airport**

**9000 Aviation Boulevard**

**Concord, N.C. 28027**

**(704) 793-9000 (phone)**

**(704) 793-1216 (fax)**

**From Charlotte, take I-85 north toward Concord to Exit 49 (Speedway Boulevard). Turn right and go 1.89 miles. The street brings you to the front of the Smith Tower.**

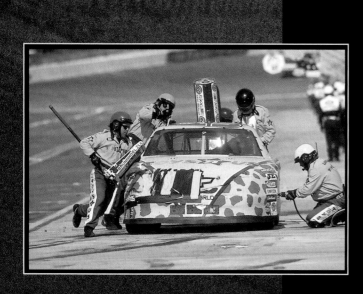

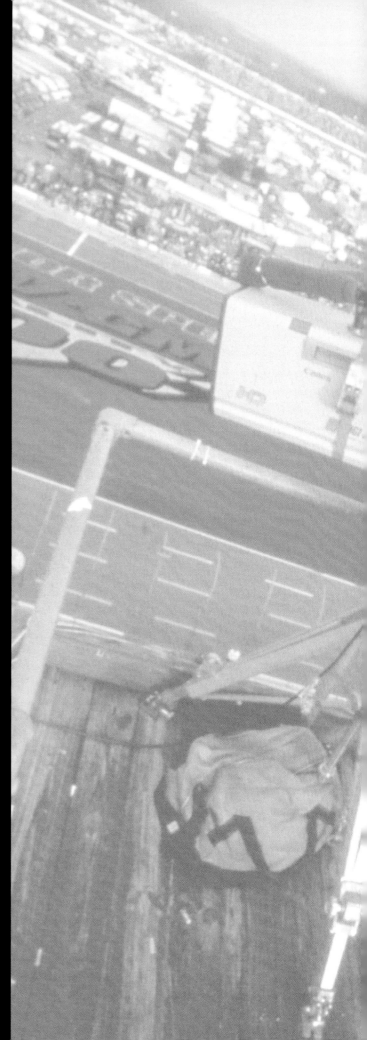

FOODS

Nearby **Concord Mills Mall** has a huge food court as well as specialty restaurants, including the Alabama Grill, named for the country music group (704 979-3000). **The Sandwich Construction Company** is an occasional driver hangout and was the place Tom Cruise visited while filming *Days of Thunder* (7801 University City Boulevard, 704 597-0008).

**The Speedway Club**, on the sixth floor of the Smith Tower at the track, is on the upper end of dining (reservations, 704 455-3216). In Charlotte, **Southend Brewery & Smokehouse**, at 2100 South Boulevard, is a restaurant that attracts families (paper tablecloths and a cup of crayons to play with) as well as drivers (Dale Earnhardt Jr. favors the place). Call 704 358-4677 for directions.

# SLEEPING and SEATING

## SLEEPING

## SEATING

Several major chains have hotels near the track. Lowe's has RV spaces available in the infield and at areas surrounding the speedway. **The Fleetwood facility**, just off Speedway Boulevard, offers cable, electricity, sewer and water hookups, and a picnic table.

For those who want a more child-friendly atmosphere, the family grandstand, near turn one, is a nonsmoking, no-alcohol area. All seats throughout the track are near restrooms and concessions.

# CHAPTER FOUR

# Backstage Before Showtime

**B**efore the cars take the track for each major race at Lowe's, before the national anthem and the waving of the green flag, something strange happens.

The prerace show.

Picture a gutted-out Mercedes, with a roll bar, jumping 293 feet and crash-landing into a pile of junk cars. Picture an RV sprinting off a ramp to jump 100 portable toilets. Picture track president and general manager H. A. "Humpy" Wheeler and his co-conspirator, Jay Howard, brainstorming the next great thriller.

"The whole reason for the prerace show is Humpy came up with the idea to help get traffic into the track earlier," says Jerry Gappens of the PR department. "He can get 40,000 to 50,000 cars into the track [area] and get them to tailgate earlier [before the show]. One, they get additional entertainment, and two, he's helping with congestion."

The concept originated when Wheeler was a child and a race fan.

"I've always been a race fan, since I was seven years old," Wheeler says.

"And I would get to races, and get there ahead of time, and nothing was happening. … We wanted something besides the parade lap. So we [at LMS] started doing stunt shows, and people liked it. We started our first military invasion in 1982 or '83, with a reenactment of [the battle on the island of] Grenada, with some liberty."

For that, members of the 82nd Airborne dropped from the sky and "captured" the speedway. Then they shot off 105 howitzers. The windows shook. "The people, uh, really liked that," Wheeler says.

The May race, being around Memorial Day weekend, always has a military theme.

One time, Wheeler recalls, helicopters dropped troops in and came back to pick them up on a swing rope. "This thing snatches them right up, and the guys literally were picked right up and taken to the airport, about eight miles from here, just dangling from this helicopter [in a harness].

"They got the ride of their lives. I thought that was pretty interesting."

At Lowe's, the tailgating takes place in the days before the race. "Come race day, they come in and see what's happening so they don't miss it," Wheeler says.

The first prerace spectacle that Howard produced for Lowe's Motor Speedway was a three-ring circus.

"Complete with elephants," Howard says. That was 18 years ago. From then on, it just got weirder.

Wheeler is known for his prerace antics, his wild promotions and his obsession with setting world records. Howard, who owns and operates JHE Production Group in Concord, across the street from the speedway, is Wheeler's partner in prerace hysteria.

"I was Humpy's gofer all four years of college," Howard says. "I would cut a week of college [at Appalachian State], come down to the speedway on race week, follow him around and run errands. I did it each race all four years of school. Then when I got out of school, he hired me full-time."

Planning a prerace spectacle can begin six months to a year ahead of time. The idea has to be carefully crafted, consist of something

that can be assembled and dismantled quickly, and be something that can fit into the time window allowed by live television.

"There is a beginning budget. But you can spend $100,000 at a race track quick," Howard says. "And you cannot impact the race. So whatever you're doing, it needs to be removed quickly, leaving nothing behind—no ruts in the grass, no broken-down staging. And that's where we've been successful in building credibility with NASCAR and with television.

"We have to say, yes, we can be ready in 10 minutes. Yes, we'll be ready for your cue."

And the stunt has to fit the venue of a 1.5-mile speedway with spectators everywhere.

"There are some core functions that any program at the speedway has to have," Howard says. "It has to be big, loud, colorful and moving. It's probably bigger than the Rose Bowl. You have an audience that's 2,000 feet wide, and you have to play to that audience."

Howard's second show with Wheeler and the speedway had a bit of a problem. "Now that I'm a dad, I can't imagine trying to take 3,200 kids on a field trip again," Howard recalls.

The idea was to have the world's largest marching band. So Wheeler and Howard rounded up 40 high school bands—3,200 youngsters—to play the October race.

"So they start fainting and passing out, and they're dropping like flies," Gappens says.

Adds Howard, "It was about 100 degrees on the track. And some of them had on brand new wool uniforms. They played one song, and a couple of kids fainted. We told the band director to play the second song, and now we've got about 25 kids on the ground."

"Humpy," says Gappens, "was like, 'The show must go on.' But after the third call over the radio, he says 'The show must stop.'"

Says Wheeler, "That was a fiasco. We had a terrible hot spell that day. It was 84 degrees in the morning, and those poor kids started walking in those wool uniforms …"

The kids were all right, but the show ended a little less dramatically than planned: Singer Charlie Daniels came out for the finale and stood by himself to perform.

"You learn," Howard says.

One of Wheeler's favorite shows involved "Jimmy the flying Greek."

"It was the first school bus jump we had," Wheeler says. "We took an ordinary school bus, put a Winston Cup engine in it, and put the seat toward the center. He had to jump the width of a football field, 52 yards. He crashed, but he made the distance."

The bus flew over a mapped-out football field and crashed into junk cars. "You couldn't have come down on solid earth, or it would have driven the engine back into his lap," Wheeler explains. "I would have had to pay him more the next time he did it."

It was a time when the movie *Jaws* was popular, so the bus was painted accordingly. "If you think like a kid, they were thinking, 'I don't want to go to school any more,' you know?" Wheeler says.

Following the bus jump, Wheeler says, he overheard longtime *Charlotte Observer* racing writer Tom Higgins make the comment, "What are they going to do next, bring in pink elephants?"

So that's what Wheeler did. Brought in elephants. But not pink. "We were worried about the Humane Society," he says.

But for all weirdness, one of the most profound has to be the Macarena dance line. The one that took the stage from the portable toilets. One hundred of them.

"I had a guy in the parking lot for two weeks cutting out the sides of Port-a-Johns," says Howard.

The units were lined up side by side so that fans couldn't see that there no longer were sides; they were connected, like a tunnel. "You could load 100 people in there without them [the crowd[ knowing it," Howard says.

Of course, first the RV jumped the 100 portables. Then the Macarena song played.

"It was like a domino effect," Howard says. "First one door opens, then another, and another, and you had no idea … And they're doing the Macarena, and the last two guys come out in toxic waste uniforms."

Insane? Sure, but Howard also is a man who once tricked his wife, on their anniversary, into flying to St. Louis to pick out her very own Clydesdale. Her name is Emma. (The horse, not the wife.)

Howard, who lives on land he purchased from Dale Earnhardt, also has worked with the tracks in Miami, Daytona, Kansas, Talladega and at Rockingham. In his office in Concord, he has a photo wall depicting every event. Even the Rocket Man in Texas. What he does in Charlotte, he says, is different from elsewhere.

"Oh, Humpy's much more liberal," he says. "He's willing to take chances and do things on the edge."

No kidding.

**Carolina Audio**
Crankin' It Up With D.W.
NASCAR on FOX
704-282-2242

IRWIN

TRADE TOUGH
From Rough to Finish

Since 1885

IRWIN IRW

TRADE TOUGH
Rough To Finish

TRADE
From Rough

# A Day at the Races

**B**y the time the car engines roar to signal the start of a race, the grounds at Lowe's Motor Speedway have been transformed into a miniature city. Fans have settled into their own "neighborhoods," complete with the amenities they need to feel at home. There are infield communities, grandstand communities and gatherings in high-rises with glassed-in views.

"For the Coca-Cola 600, you've got 200,000 people in attendance. So what happens there is, you've got all the things you expect to see in a city of 200,000 people," says the track's Jerry Gappens. "We have a police department set up, a fire department, and the whole infrastructure of water, garbage pick-up, retail outlets."

The infield is segmented into different developments, complete with narrow roads, restroom areas and a roving sanitation truck. "You've got people sleeping in tents in a campground, and then you have the nicer neighborhoods with the self-contained motor homes, all the way up to the $1.2 million penthouse," Gappens says. "There are people at the Speedway Club eating lobster and steak, and there's the guy with the $19 ticket eating a hot dog. There is the upper echelon, with the white-collar banking community, and there are the middle-class people who are the backbone of the sport. And there are people in the infield who can afford the suites, but who choose to rough it."

## Bringing them all together takes
## months of planning.

"It's real interesting, and it's challenging, because it takes about 6,000 people to produce the event," says track president Humpy Wheeler. "From the extra police crew, to the backup mechanical people, to elevators and things like that.

"The most important people here will be the plumbers. We do the same thing the circus does when they clean up after the elephants. Only we clean up after 200,000 people."

To prepare, the staff and crew have drills to plot any possible scenario.

"The control tower is sort of bedlam on race day," Wheeler says. "You constantly, constantly have things to challenge you. But it's a very interesting challenge when you get through. The folks who work here full-time, generally the momentum of the event keeps them going for another week. Then they just totally collapse."

The staff holds a prerace meeting a few months before an event, then gathers for a postrace critique to discuss their effort and review letters from fans. An autopsy of the event, Wheeler calls it.

Gappens recalls one year in which Wheeler, during the postrace meeting, reprimanded the security crew because some-

**Jason Keller, Scott Riggs**

one was able to sneak in for free. Of course, the lecture was a case of Wheeler's easy-going humor.

"The head of security looks at him, and he looks horrified," Gappens says, "and he asks, 'But how could this happen?' Humpy says that a little baby boy had been born in an ambulance, under the grandstands at turn one. So he was joking that the little boy had gotten in for free."

Such is life in the big makeshift city.

"All things can happen like that," Gappens says. "We have everything from heart attacks to sunburn. There are a couple of hospital facilities on the site. One year, we had a gentleman have a heart attack in traffic, and a North Carolina Highway Patrol officer had a mobile defibrillator and was able to save his life.

"There are a lot of major things that go on at these events. It's bigger than the NCAA Final Four or the Masters."

Fans who frequent Lowe's take their racing seriously. The 20-by 30-foot plots in the infield are renewed annually, and the people become friends. "One guy might be from Wisconsin, and another from West Virginia, and they send each other Christmas cards and so on," Gappens says. "We had one guy who came every year with his son, kind of a father-son tradition, and when he [the father] died, they had a memorial service where he enjoyed his spot, and

**Bobby Labonte**

all his friends [in surrounding campers] spread his ashes where he watched the races. People are very passionate about this sport."

Another time, a woman was able to spread her husband's ashes in a flower bed at Victory Lane. "It's amazing what goes on, and can happen, in a race weekend," Gappens says.

Planning begins well in advance. October race preparations by the staff can start in January. So can outlines for the races the next calendar year.

It takes over 100,000 hours by these 6,000 people [on staff on race day] to produce the event," Wheeler says. "That's the real key, is planning.

"Those of us who do this for a living, it's exhilarating. Sometimes you gnash your teeth, but most of the time it's great. People are very conscious of each other, and that's why things go so well.

"Usually."

**Dale Jarrett**

Wally Dallenbach

David Green

A NUMBER OF THINGS

# CHAPTER SIX

# A Number of Things

**T**he people who run Lowe's Motor Speedway have a sense of humor. They need it. What other race track, three days before a big event, hosts something called The Great Toilet Flush? LMS does, to make sure the water supply is, well, adequate, should the more than 1,800 commodes on the premises be used at the same moment.

There was a problem with that once. Back in the late 1970s, Janet Guthrie was trying to become the first woman to race in the Indianapolis 500. So all the publicity was in Indiana, and Charlotte didn't sell out the Coca-Cola 600. When Guthrie didn't make the Indy field, CMS's Bruton Smith and Humpy Wheeler found her a ride in a stock car, and she came to Carolina.

"Sure enough, all the reporters came down to see how a woman would drive a 3,500-pound stock car in the heat of the day," says the track's Jerry Gappens. "Sure enough, she qualified, and women, by themselves, came out and started buying tickets.

"Come that Sunday, and Humpy had sold out his first-ever race, and she's running well, in the top 20, and Humpy's brother, David, comes in and says, 'We got a big problem. We're about to run out of water.'"

What the track hadn't planned for was a simple mathematical equation: Having a large crowd of women equals a large amount of bath-

room use. The well was about to run dry. Wheeler was faced with fire safety concerns and sanitary concerns. He told track officials to *please* not throw a caution flag (automatic bathroom break) until he could pipe in some more water.

The event led to a major capital improvement program at the track, which now boasts that nearly 40 percent of its audience is women, whereas before Janet Guthrie, it had been 15 percent.

Here, courtesy of the track's public relations department, are other pieces of useful information. Just in case anyone should ask.

USEFUL INFORMATION

***There*** are more than 130 flagpoles on the speedway's property.

***During*** the UAW-GM Quality 500 race in the fall, the track sets out almost 7,000 trash cans and collects more than 400 tons of trash.

***Three*** 30-foot truckloads of paper products, such as paper towels and toilet paper (see above) are used on race days.

***Not*** one to leave a bad impression, the track spends nearly $750,000 a year on landscaping.

*The* speedway grounds crews use 35 tractors and 21 lawn mowers to keep the more than 2,000 acres looking good enough for a Kodak moment.

*On* the day of the fall race, the speedway becomes North Carolina's fourth largest city, with the nearly 200,000 people in attendance placing little Concord just behind Charlotte, Raleigh and Greensboro.

*It* takes 6,000 people and more than 100,000 hours of work to make the UAW-GM Quality 500 a reality. Statistically, that's twice the effort of putting on a Super Bowl.

*Once* upon a time, the land now occupied by LMS was a plantation during the Civil War.

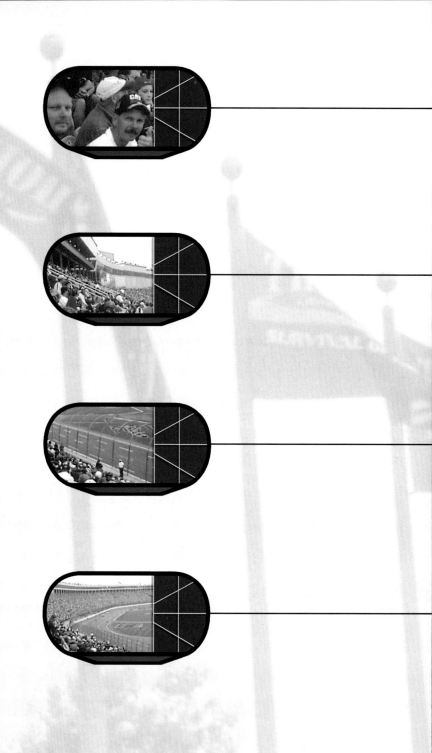

*Not* only that, but, going back further, George Washington ate lunch and rested in a house that at one time served as the speedway's offices.

*The* small, one-fifth-mile oval located outside the turn three tunnel is known as "Outback Speedway." Because it is located "out back."

*The* inner perimeter road around LMS is named Darrell Waltrip Way in honor of the three-time NASCAR Winston Cup champion.

*In* 1960, Lowe's (then Charlotte Motor Speedway) became the first track to host a 600-mile NASCAR-sanctioned event. The Coca-Cola 600 still is the longest on the circuit.

**In** 1984, Lowe's became the only sports facility in the United States to offer year-round living accommodations, with 40 condominiums going up for sale above turn one.

**When** the Speedway Club opened in 1988, it was the first exclusive members-only private club at a motorsports facility. The perks: a 240-seat restaurant, ballroom seating for 400, and a 3,741-seat enclosed clubhouse. The Club occupies two stories of the Smith Tower, which also houses administrative offices, ticket operations, a gift shop and leased office space.

**In** 1992, thanks to Musco Lighting of Oskaloosa, Iowa, LMS became the first modern superspeedway to host night racing. The lighting system has 1,200 permanent lighting fixtures and cost $1.7 million.

*Who's* on first? Drivers who made their NASCAR Winston Cup debut at Lowe's include Dale Earnhardt Jr. (1999 Coca-Cola 600), Jeremy Mayfield (1993 UAW-GM Quality 500), Michael Waltrip (1985 Coca-Cola 600), Brett Bodine (1986 Coca-Cola 600), and Dale Earnhardt (1974 Coca-Cola 600).

*Knowing* a good left turn when he sees one, Darrell Waltrip made his 700th career Winston Cup Series start in the 1997 Coca-Cola 600.

*Who* needs an engine? On April 3, 2001, Chris Harkey, one of the nation's top amateur cyclists, established an outdoor world record for miles completed on a bicycle in a 12-hour period when he covered 276.37 miles (192.72 laps) around a 1.434-mile course on the inside of the superspeedway. The distance, in a straight line, would have taken Harkey from Charlotte to Richmond, Virginia.

**"I'm** amazed I'm not crying right now. I'm a pretty emotional guy, and to do it at Charlotte... my worst race track. I learned a lot in that car yesterday."

*—Rookie Jamie McMurray,*
*after winning the 2002 UAW-GM Qual-*

# CHAPTER SEVEN

# He Said, She Said

They like the location, but they dislike the track. Or they like the track, but not in sunny weather. Opinions vary. Here's what some drivers have to say about racing at Lowe's Motor Speedway.

"**I'll** tell you what, I'm real excited about next week, because on long runs we've got a great car."

—*Tony Stewart,*
*before the 2001 Coca-Cola 600*

"**Charlotte** is a hit-or-miss track. The weather plays a big part. If the track is hot, it's slick, and that will loosen the car up. On the other hand, a cloud cover will make the car stick better, which means you're going faster. You've also got a bump between turns three and four that makes things interesting, too. Basically, you just never know what to expect when you race at Charlotte."

—*Jack Sprague*

**"Charlotte** is one of those tracks that makes me happy I sit on the box and call the shots rather than drive. You just never know what you're getting into until the race starts. Even then, things can change drastically in one lap. Every corner is different, and you can't run too low in them or you'll upset the car."

—*Dennis Connor,*
*Sprague's former*
*crew chief*

**"We** definitely put on a great show for them under the lights at Lowe's, but it can be a very nerve-wracking race for the drivers."

—*Ward Burton*

**"This** race track is pretty tricky, and if you hit the bumps going through [turns] three and four it seems like if your car is loose, you get really loose. If you're tight, you get really tight. I hit the bumps and just couldn't hold it on the bottom. If I can keep my car on the bottom in the center, I can drive off pretty much wide open and not even get close to the wall."

—*Jamie McMurray*

**"Charlotte** is not as bad as some of the other tracks. Aero[dynamics] does play a role, but Charlotte is still a handling race track. You've got to get your car to drive well and handle well. That's the main thing at Charlotte. It has more bumps than some of these other tracks do, and that's what can change the attitude of your race car."

—*Tony Stewart*

**Kevin Harvick, Jimmie Johnson**

"**Lowe's** is one of my favorite race tracks,

and we've had a lot of success there."

—*Jimmie Johnson*

**"I** love racing here at home. Charlotte has been

a place where we've run really, really well,

but other than The Winston, we don't have

the finishes to prove it. [In the 2002 spring

race] we were just chillin' ..."

—*Dale Earnhardt Jr.*

**"Charlotte** is where you compromise your setups for the time of day so that you can run halfway decent for the first third of the race and really go to town the second half of the race. ... The surface knows the difference. It changes all the time. It's the only track I know of where you hope to 'catch a cloud' during qualifying at night because the moonlight changes the asphalt. On race day, man, it's a whole different world."

—*Kyle Petty*

**"Used** to be, the 600 was the big, big race at Charlotte because it was the longest one. It was the one with all the prestige. ... The weird part is I don't know if there's that much difference from a driver's standpoint in 600 miles and 500 miles. It takes a lot physically to go 600 miles, but believe me, it can take a lot to go 500 miles, too."

*—Kyle Petty*

**Bobby Labonte**

**"I've** won some big races, but I know when I look back at my career it won't seem complete without a trophy from Charlotte. I like racing at Charlotte."

—*Ricky Rudd,*
*who has 25 top*
*tens at the track*
*without a victory*

**"Going** back and racing at Charlotte is like being home, but you are still at the race track all day. ... The nice thing about being close to home is a lot of evenings you can go home and be able to put the kids to bed. If the schedule works out, you can even drop the kids off at school and still make it to the track for practice."

—*John Andretti*

**"The** track feels fairly flat when you're in a race car. You're pushing the limit when you're driving the car, and there's never enough banking. There isn't even enough banking at Bristol, and that track is like a bowl."

*—John Andretti*

**"Charlotte** is a fun track to race on and is a place I enjoy racing. Aside from that, pretty much everyone gets to spend some time at home for a weekend."

*—Dale Jarrett,*
*who has three*
*wins at Lowes*

**"Charlotte** has been real good to me. It's been one of my favorite places. I love the place. It's definitely been a good track for me."

—*Jeremy Mayfield*

**"The** best thing about racing at Charlotte is being able to be at home all week. We have a lot of friends and family that come into town for the race, and between myself and all my brothers, we have extremely full houses."

—*Kenny Wallace*

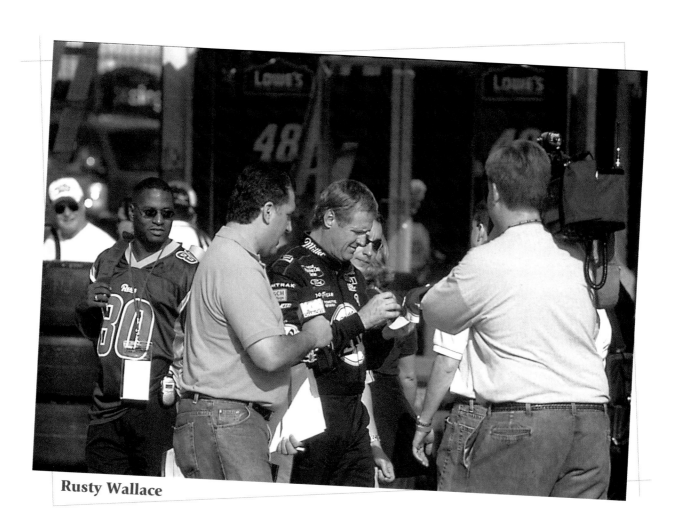

**Rusty Wallace**

**"People** always want to know what my favorite track is, and Charlotte is definitely one of the tracks at the top of my list. I think that is one of everybody's favorites because this is our home turf. Charlotte is a fun track anyway, because it changes so much during the course of the weekend. It makes for a challenging and grueling day for everyone on the team."

*—Ken Schrader*

**"An** early draw will definitely hurt you, because the track is real sensitive to weather. If you get an early draw, it will affect your times— the track will slow you down. The track starts to speed up, but then toward the end of the night it starts to slow down again, because the moisture makes the track slick. If you can get a draw right in the middle, I think that's when the track is best."

*—Casey Atwood*

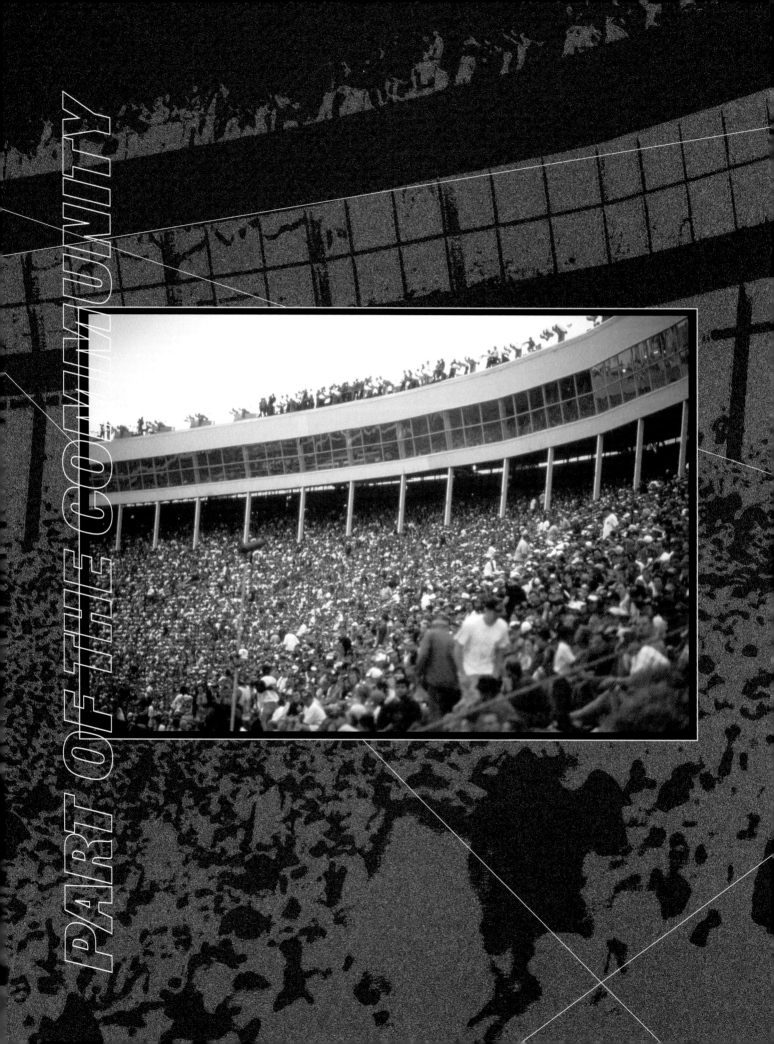

PART OF THE COMMUNITY

# CHAPTER EIGHT

# Part of the Community

There is one stoplight on Route 73 in Huntersville, North Carolina, a town next to Concord, where traffic is exceptionally heavy on race days. But track officials have managed to alleviate that, with a little help from their friends.

"The Huntersville police do a good job to help us," says track president Humpy Wheeler. "And if they didn't, traffic would be backed up there for 20 miles."

It's that kind of cooperation from the community that symbolizes how Lowe's Motor Speedway works with, and is helped by, the areas it affects.

"We feel we need to give something back," Wheeler says. "Most of the people who help us, we help them back."

Perhaps the most visible way Lowe's donates to the area is through Speedway Children's Charities, founded in 1984 by track

owner Bruton Smith. The non-profit organization has chapters at each of Speedway Motorsports' six tracks and has raised more than $5 million, including $1.2 million in 2000. In 2001, the Charities gave more than $1.3 million to 286 non-profit children's groups, representing more than 190,000 youngsters.

What began as a formal ball the week of the Coca-Cola 600 as the organization's sole fundraiser has grown to be a cluster of events built around race weeks with a ratio of one staff member to 122 volunteers.

In other race cities, the Charities gather support through such things as memorabilia auctions, golf tournaments and interactive events with fun walks, cookouts and track garage tours.

"The Children's Charities is an arm of the track, and we spend time and money to promote that as much as we can, to raise money for the Charities," Wheeler says.

The year-round fundraising effort distributed more than $450,000 in checks to help children in Mecklenburg and Cabbarus counties during the 2002 Christmas season, estimates Jerry Gappens of the promotions department. The Lowe's chapter lists 54 local beneficiaries, including children's homes, cultural centers, hospice chapters and learning centers.

"Obviously with the presence we have in the community, just with the size and impact we have in this area, people look to you to help," Gappens says.

The track helps in other ways, too, such as sponsoring other sports events in the area and providing a way for youth groups to help themselves.

"We give free tickets to the Boy Scouts and Girl Scouts during the NASCAR Busch race, for example, and they wear their uniforms and are admitted free to the family grandstand," Gappens says.

The executive staff also lends its time to various civic organizations, and on race days, clubs are invited to help run the concession booths and help, in return for a donation from the track.

Gappens estimates that in 2002, more than $1 million was paid to different groups for their labor. "It could be band boosters, an AAU basketball team—a lot of these groups utilize the event to get finances. They work the concession stands. That's very prominent. They get paid a flat fee, and the parents do it," he says.

Says Wheeler, "The community has been very good to us overall. People in Concord, Charlotte and Gastonia have benefited from us, but they certainly help us out.

"People have to put up with the traffic, particularly in May. People can't open things [businesses] on Sundays [because of the congestion]; people can't do things on Sundays.

"And I think we need to put back into the community."

# CHAPTER NINE

# The Last Lap

The sport of NASCAR has come so far since the modern era began that it's difficult to imagine what it will look like in another 30 years.

In 1972, the Grand National Series became known as Winston Cup when the R. J. Reynolds company began sponsorship of a points fund for drivers, worth $100,000.

When Dale Earnhardt won his first Winston Cup championship in 1980, he pocketed $588,926. In 2002, Winston Cup champion Tony Stewart earned $4,695,150.

Faster cars, marketing deals, television and endorsements have expanded the sport away from the deep South into a nationwide, even global, business. Small-town tracks, such as North Wilkesboro, are being pushed aside in favor of ultra-modern facilities in such places as Chicago and Las Vegas.

So, what of Charlotte, which hosted its first race more than 40 years ago? With two Winston Cup dates, The Winston All-Star race and its status as the hometown track of many drivers, Lowe's Motor Speedway seems a safe bet to hang around for that next 30 years.

"I would say this: that if you take the speedway and combine it with the 300 race shops that are within 100 miles of the speedway, I think all of us are proud of the fact that this has become a significant industry not only to this area, but to the whole state," says track president Humpy Wheeler.

"As we continue to change from the tobacco, textile and furniture economy [in North Carolina], this [racing] is one of the things that has helped make up the loss in those industries. And I think it's going to continue to grow."

Wheeler has a vision for the future at LMS. He sees more grandstand seating. Even, maybe, another Winston Cup date.

"We've got room to put a significant amount of grandstands in the backstretch and down the third turn," Wheeler says. "We

could get 80,000 seats in those areas if we had to, but we might have to tear down some of the original seats from 1960."

To stay competitive, he says, the track might have to do that. Seating, he believes, is as much a factor as location in keeping race dates.

"The problem is, it's not so much the market, it's how many seats you've got," he says. "Take Bristol [built in 1961 with 18,000 seats]. It's one of the strongest facilities in NASCAR, with over 140,000 seats. Richmond [originally built in 1946] is up there, at almost 100,000 seats. Martinsville has a new addition that's going to put them at more than 88,000."

Small towns, big tracks.

"And the purses have risen dramatically in the last five years," he says. "Hopefully that should calm down.

"But I see this place here [Lowe's] having as many seats as Indy, which is in excess of 250,000, because the Coca-Cola 600 does extremely well and is one of the top three racing events in the country."

The Winston also does well and has become synonymous with Charlotte and the race festivities of the city.

"Looking forward the next 10 or 15 years, I think the sport of NASCAR racing is going to continue to escalate in the major markets. I think you'll see races move. I think we'll be one of the only Winston Cup tracks to have two, maybe three race dates."

Wheeler says "we" for a reason.

"People start asking, 'How long you going to do it?'" he says of the possibility of retirement.

Wheeler will turn 65 in 2003.

"But as long as I've got my health and it continues to be fun, I'll probably keep doing it for a while."

# Celebrate the Heroes of Stock Car Racing
## in These Other Acclaimed Titles from Sports Publishing.

**Matt Kenseth:**
*Above and Beyond*
by Kelley Maruszewski
(Matt Kenseth's sister)

- 10 x 10 hardcover
- 160 pages
- color photos throughout
- $24.95
- 2003 release!

**StockcarToons 2:**
*More Grins and Spins on the*
*Winston Cup Circuit*
by Mike Smith, editorial cartoonist
for the *Las Vegas Sun*

- 11 x 8.5 softcover • 160 pages
- cartoons throughout
- $12.95 • 2003 release!

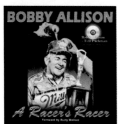

**Bobby Allison:**
*A Racer's Racer*
by Bobby Allison with
Tim Packman

- 10 x 10 hardcover
- 160 pages
- color photos throughout
- Includes an audio CD!
- $29.95
- 2003 release!

**Tony Stewart:**
*High Octane in the Fast Lane*
by The Associated Press
and AP/Wide World Photos

- 10 x 10 hardcover • 160 pages
- color photos throughout
- Includes a 60-minute audio CD!
- $39.95
- 2003 release!

**Atlanta Motor Speedway:**
*A Weekend at the Track*
by Kathy Persinger

- 8.5 x 11 hardcover
- 128 pages
- color photos throughout
- $24.95
- 2003 release!

**As They Head for the Checkers:**
*Fantastic Finishes, Memorable Milestones and*
*Heroes Remembered from the World of Racing*
by Kathy Persinger & Mark Garrow (audio)

- 10 x 10 hardcover • 160 pages
- 100 color and b/w photos throughout
- Includes an audio CD!
- $39.95
- 2003 release!

**Along for the Ride**
by Larry Woody

- 5.5 x 8 1/4 hardcover
- 191 pages
- photos throughout
- $19.95
- 2003 release!

**Sterling Marlin: The Silver Bullet**
by Larry Woody

- 8.5 x 11 hardcover • 128 pages
- 100 color photos throughout
- Includes a cdracecard CD-ROM!
- $29.95

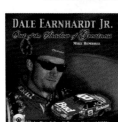

**Dale Earnhardt Jr.: Out of**
*the Shadow of Greatness*
by Mike Hembree

- 10 x 10 hardcover
- 160 pages
- color photos throughout
- Includes a 60-minute audio CD!
- $39.95 • 2003 release!

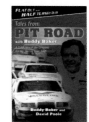

**Flat Out and Half Turned**
*Over: Tales from Pit Road*
*with Buddy Baker*
by Buddy Baker with David Poole

- 5.5 x 8.25 hardcover
- 169 pages
- photos throughout
- $19.95

**Jeff Gordon:**
*Burning Up the Track*
by the Indianapolis Star

- 10 x 10 hardcover
- 160 pages
- color photos throughout
- Includes a 60-minute audio CD!
- $39.95
- 2003 release!

**The History of America's Greatest**
*Stock Car Tracks: From Daytona*
*to the Brickyard*
by Kathy Persinger

- Oversized hardcover in the shape of
a racetrack • 160 pages
- 100 color and b/w photos throughout
- $29.95

To order at any time, please call toll-free **1-877-424-BOOK (2665)**.
For fast service and quick delivery, order on-line at **www.SportsPublishingLLC.com**.